SNOHOMISH CARNEGIE: A LEGACY RESTORED

DATE DUE			
OCT 0 2			
JAN 2 0 1978			

Copyright © Taylor Russell 2024

All rights reserved.

Produced in partnership with the Snohomish Carnegie Foundation.

Published in the United States by SnohomishWalks. For questions about this book, please write to hello@snohomishwalks.com.

*Old and young, zealous students, and
seekers after mere amusement,
in good clothes and in poor ones,
a constant procession through the doors...*

*Each of them gets something
more than a book...*

*It is our community center which we are apt
to take for granted... daily doing a great share,
building up the minds of people
that they may be better citizens.*

SNOHOMISH TRIBUNE, 1925

HISTORY OF THE SNOHOMISH CARNEGIE LIBRARY
Coming Together ... 11
Growth & Resilience ... 25
Modern Changes ... 35

LIBRARIAN BIOGRAPHIES, 1873 TO 1973
Eldridge Morse ... 41
Emma Patric ... 42
Grace Pineo ... 42
Mary Mitchell ... 43
Doris Mitchell ... 43
Catharine McMurchy ... 44
Ethel Cloes ... 44
Marie Sweet ... 45
Mildred Dean ... 45
Geraldine Earls ... 46
Lillian Trapp ... 47
Evalyn Klein ... 48

SUPPLEMENTARY HISTORICAL MATERIAL ... 49

ACKNOWLEDGEMENTS ... 99

SNOHOMISH needed a library. The small riverside settlement was growing rapidly. The year was 1900 and the town had just crested 2,000 residents. Buoyed by bustling lumber and agricultural industries, the population was on track to double within the next decade.

At the helm of the community's drive for improvement was Adell Thompson, an Iowa transplant and the wife of local doctor Thomas Thompson. Known for her dedication and ambitious ideas, she was the newly elected leader of the Cosmopolitan Club, a social club that started as a mother's support group and grew into a Women's Book Club. It had rebranded itself "Cosmopolitan" to reflect the group's new mission: to beautify and improve life in small town Snohomish.

In ensuing years, the club would successfully lobby for domestic science classes, public water fountains, and individual towels in local schools (they had previously been communal). However, at the dawn of the 20th century, Snohomish's most pressing need was undoubtedly a library. The book club had outgrown the sparse room they rented on First Street. Poorly lit by dim oil lamps, the space felt cramped and awkward within a maze of donated books. The club imagined a different kind of space: large, open, stately, and inviting.

* * *

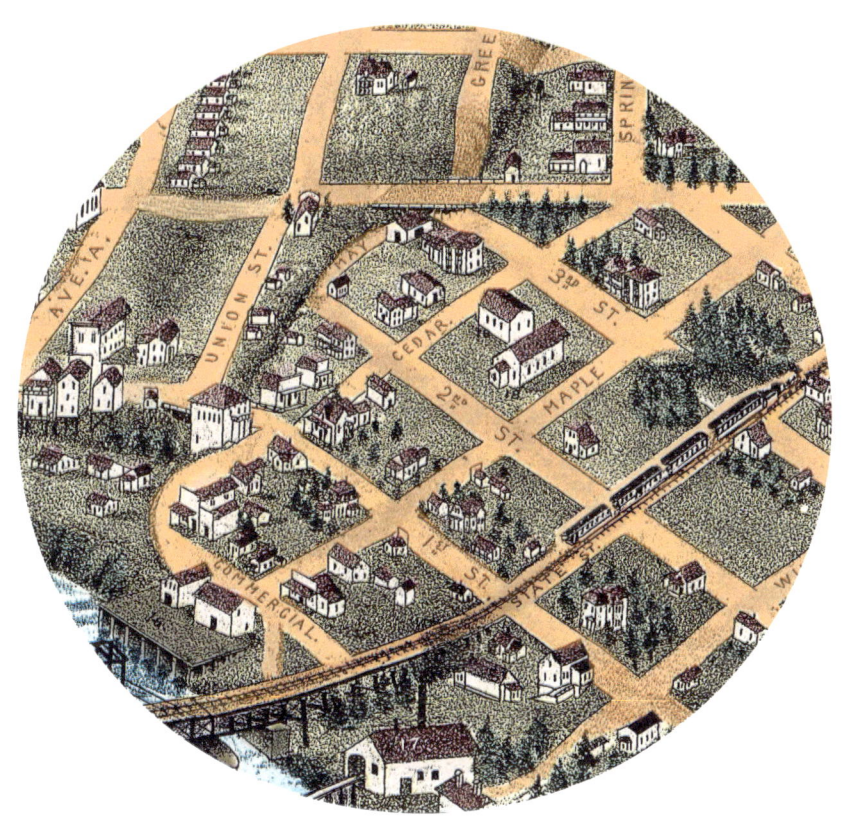

Bird's eye view of East Snohomish, 1890.

Coming Together

The desire for a proper city library emerged almost as soon as the town was platted. In June 1871, homesteader Emory Ferguson filed paperwork christening the town Snohomish, after the local people who called themselves "Sdoh-doh-hobsch." He transformed the raw land into an orderly network of numbered streets and lettered avenues.

On a chilly November evening in 1873, a group gathered at the home of Eldridge Morse, a young lawyer and Snohomish's first. He and Albert Folsom, the town's first doctor, proposed forming a subscription-based literary society. Members could either pay $25 for a lifetime membership or $3 per month and gain access to the entire membership's pool of privately-owned books and collections. This included encyclopedias, science textbooks, and classical works in Greek and Latin, as well as rare fossils, taxidermied specimens, and ethnological artifacts. Additionally, members received a monthly handwritten newsletter, the Shillalah, featuring book reviews, local gossip, and thinkpieces on self-improvement, science, and philosophy.

THE ATHENEUM HALL, BEFORE BEING SCRAPPED
AND REPLACED WITH THE CATHCART BUILDING.

*"All of them poor and struggling,
cut off from the great world of books and newspapers
and colleges and schools, without churches;
leading lives in manual toil and surrounded by the
rough, boisterous life which the logging camp invited
but still, craving knowledge and intellectual activity
and, with scant resources, founding an institution,
creating a museum of real value and finally building
the first edifice dedicated to such a purpose in the
entire Northwest..."*

WILLIAM WHITFIELD, 1926

The newcomers supported the idea and the society was named "Atheneum," a nod to Ancient Greek devotees of Athena, the goddess of wisdom and the arts. By 1876, the society had enough memberships from throughout the county to purchase its own plot of land and to construct a two-story home for its collections. The Atheneum building, at the corner of First Street and Avenue D, opened its doors on September 14, 1877.[*] This was the first library and museum in Snohomish County.[**]

Within a year, the finances of the Atheneum Society began to falter. The country was grappling with an economic downtown, spurred by dwindling railroad investment and stricter bank lending practices. The depression was slow to hit Snohomish, but it did and especially impacted the pocketbooks of Morse and other Atheneum founders. Loans extended by its members to local investors soured, leading to defaults.

With reduced income, unable to meet maintenance costs, the society had no choice but to abandon their building. It gradually fell into disrepair. A few years later, the building inspector condemned it, prompting local lumberman Isaac Cathcart to purchase it. He hoped to renovate it into a music hall. The Atheneum's treasures, including the inaugural piece of lumber from the town's first sawmill, were scattered.[***] Some items went back into private hands and others were donated to the Territorial

---

[*] Lumber was donated by the Port Blakely Mill Company. The mill's owners had sued a group of Snohomish loggers, defendants of Eldridge Morse. After illuminating the mill's unjust accounting methods, Morse was able to settle the case for half of what the mill sought. The mill also agreed to donate lumber to Morse's civic structure.

[**] The Snohomish Atheneum was the second community library in the state. The first opened in Steilacoom in 1858. The Washington Territorial Library formed in 1853, becoming the first official library in the area.

[***] The Bennett & Witter Mill began operation in 1876. Located on the Pilchuck River, Emory Ferguson was a part owner. He then sold it to his father-in-law, Hiram D. Morgan, who operated it as the Morgan Brothers Lumber & Shingle Mill.

University (later the University of Washington). The building was dismantled in 1910 and replaced by a one-story brick retail space.

The wives of the Atheneum members worked hard to preserve the pioneer legacy of wisdom and learning. They safeguarded the group's literature and, in 1896, opened a small reading room on First Street. Open to the public free of charge, it was stocked with the society's newspapers, magazines, and around 500 remaining books. Designating themselves the Women's Book Club, they kept records and managed reader's activity in the small space. Though well used, it struggled for existence, reliant on the generosity of early pioneers to pay the rent. In September 1900, citizens petitioned the city for a monthly allocation of $15 from the city treasury to maintain the reading room.

With or without municipal support, the women of Snohomish were committed to improving the community's access to knowledge. Many of them hailed from the East and from urban environments with more refinement and high culture than could be found in the Pacific Northwest wilderness. The group attracted determined women whose husbands provided both financial and emotional support, as businessmen and advisors with a shared vision for progress.

With the aim of establishing a new library, Mrs. Thompson and Mrs. Charles Robinson formed a sub-committee to solicit donations and support. They enlisted local attorney John Watterson Miller for legal counsel. After hosting a few fundraising events, mainly dinners with music and dancing, they found themselves with $1,500 in donated cash and a public eager to support their work.

From the windows of her newly finished Victorian on the northeast corner of Pearl and Cedar Streets, Mrs. Thompson looked onto an unsightly, dilapidated structure. Constructed in 1875, in recent years the home across the street had become overgrown and was seldom occupied. The home belonged to Mrs. Emma Jackson, daughter of early

THE ORIGINAL JACKSON HOME ON LIBRARY PROPERTY. THIS IMAGE WAS SENT IN WITH THE CARNEGIE GRANT APPLICATION.

settler John Bakeman and wife of Henry Jackson. The Jackson family were significant land owners in early Snohomish, buying up much of the east end of First Street. Daniel Jackson, Emma's father-in-law, had established the town's first wharf, at the foot of today's Cady Park. Later, he founded the Washington Steamboat & Transportation Company and the family amassed a considerable fortune. He and his sons developed the Alcazar Theatre and other buildings in Snohomish. By the turn of the century Daniel and most of his descendants had moved to Seattle and their family home sat empty.*

Mrs. Thompson recognized an opportunity to put the property to better use. She promptly wrote to Mrs. Jackson and discovered her and Henry struggling under a burden of unpaid taxes. Seizing

---

* The lots originally belonged to Mary Low, wife of Woodbury Sinclair. She sold them to Charles Jackson on February 15, 1876 for $125. Charles sold it to his brother Henry on April 11, 1877 for $400. An 1892 document shows the property sold "for delinquent city taxes for the year 1892." Yet, in 1895, Henry again owned the property. It would seem delinquent taxes were a habitual problem.

Mayor Gilbert Turner, wife Rose and children in 1904. They lived next door to the modern Blackman Museum.

the chance, the Cosmopolitan Club offered to settle taxes on the couple's behalf, if Mrs. Jackson would donate the property for use as a city library. She agreed, and the Club issued a check totalling $792.17 to the county authorities. In July 1901, the Jacksons formally transferred ownership of the western half of the block to the Club, via the Thompsons. To their surprise, county commissioner T.E. Skaggs learned about the plans for the library and waived the back taxes, refunding the Club's payment. Mr. Miller assisted in clearing the title pro bono. The land was secured.

The Club packed up their reading room and moved across First Street into the former Jackson home. Renovations began to remove walls and open up the downstairs, creating one large reading room. Long tables and chairs filled the space, with a separate book room behind. This was lined with sturdy bookshelves crafted from local lumber. A small office at the back of the house was set aside for the librarian's use.

A formal dedication ceremony took place on July 12, 1901. As admission, attendees brought books to donate to the reading room. Local publisher and state representative Charles Gorham delivered an address to an audience sitting amidst orchard trees on the spacious lawn. Mayor Gilbert Turner formally accepted the library on behalf of the city, and an invocation was given by Reverend C. L. Mears. The event ran past dusk, but attendees marveled at the bright bulbs strung high above, powered by Snohomish's new electrical plant. Such lights would be a welcome change from candles and oil lamps, particularly because the reading room had extended its hours to 9 a.m. to 9 p.m. Monday through Friday.

Before the ink had dried on the library deal, Mrs. Thompson had identified the ideal candidate for the city's first librarian. Initially hesitant, Mrs. Emma Patric eventually accepted the position at Mrs. Thompson's insistence. With university degrees, Mrs. Patric was the most qualified woman for the job and would be able to organize and establish proper library systems from the ground up. In her first month of work, Mrs. Patric purchased accession and catalog books, book pockets "printed with the rules for book room," and other necessary office items. She worked long hours and was paid in lodging. She and her new husband, Arthur, lived in an apartment in the north end of the library.

To supplement the costs of furnishing the new space, the Cosmopolitan Club again hosted fundraising dinners. Mrs. Patric recalled clearing the magazines and newspapers from the reading room tables to make space for large banquet-style parties. Between 1902 and 1910, the Club raised $2,673.39. The money was

ANDREW CARNEGIE
2 EAST 91ST STREET
NEW YORK

April 6, 1909

E. Thistlethwaite, Esq.,
    City Clerk,
        Snohomish, Wash.

Dear Sir,

  Yours of March 30th receivd. When Mr. Carnegie sees plans which can be approved by him for a Library Bilding which can be erected, complete, redy for occupancy and for the purpose intended within the amount promist, arrangements will be made for payments on the bilding as work progresses.

       Respectfully yours,

       Ja. Bertram

       P. Secretary.

LETTER FROM CARNEGIE'S SECRETARY, REGARDING GRANT TERMS.

used for purchasing books, undertaking structural repairs, and hiring the town's second librarian, Mary Mitchell, who began her duties in 1907.

In 1903, the Snohomish Library Association was formed. William Dolsen served as president alongside Wilson McNeill and George Cochran. Their objective was to oversee the library's finances and to draft a compelling application to the Carnegie Foundation. They hoped to be awarded a grant to replace the modified library-house with a bigger, more modern public building. Neighboring Everett had received $25,000 through such a grant that same year, thanks to the enterprising Everett Women's Book Club. Snohomish desired the same.

At that time, Andrew Carnegie was the wealthiest man in the world. He had billions of dollars from the steel industry and other prescient investments. Growing up in poverty with a passion for reading, he was inspired to give back to those on their own quests for self-education.[*] The first library Carnegie funded was in his hometown of Dunfermline, Scotland in 1883. He then established a foundation to build them across America. When Carnegie died in 1919, he had successfully completed 2,500 libraries, at a cost of over $1.3 billion. The state of Washington had 33 Carnegie libraries built, with grants averaging $15,000 to $36,000. The first was in Seattle in 1901.[**]

Snohomish's initial attempts to apply for a Carnegie grant were unsuccessful. In July 1903, the Library Association sent in its

---

[*] Carnegie believed the wealthy owed debts to society that must be repaid. In an 1889 essay, he wrote, "The man who dies rich dies disgraced." Upon his death in 1919, he had divested 95% of his fortune, leaving his widow and children with relatively little to inherit.

[**] Carnegie granted an astonishing $200,000 for the Seattle library. Previously housed in the Yesler Mansion, the structure and all 25,000 of the library's books had been lost in a fire on January 2, 1901. Carnegie announced his gift to Seattle just 5 days later.

first handwritten two-page application, including pictures of the Jackson home and grounds. Carnegie's secretary, James Bertram, wrote back that the facilities seemed plenty large enough for a town of Snohomish's size. Mr. Dolsen responded that the census numbers Bertram referenced were out-of-date and no longer accurate. He heard nothing.

The Cosmopolitan Club persisted, canvassing the town house-to-house with a petition to demonstrate the need for a proper library. These signatures, along with a new application and a promise of $500 a year towards library upkeep, were forwarded to Carnegie's office in October 1906. Still they were refused. Bertram wrote, "If $500 a year is all the City can pledge for carrying on a Library, that would not carry on much more than can be done in the present building." He suggested the city repurpose the living accommodations that were used by Mrs. Patric into additional library space.

Frustrated by the terse refusals, Emory Ferguson requested his friend Senator Samuel Piles come tour the present library and help their cause. Piles hailed from Kentucky, but had moved to Snohomish in 1883 after earning his law degree. He was renowned as "a polished orator and a settled reasoner" as he took up court cases for early county settlers. In 1904 he had successfully earned a seat in the United State Senate.

Senator Piles did visit, and upon his return to Washington, D.C., he began a relentless letter-writing campaign to Carnegie's secretary. He strongly urged Bertram to grant the library funds, pledging, "Snohomish has a splendid future, and Mr. Carnegie will never regret making the donation which its citizens request." A month later, he wrote, "I am firmly convinced that Mr. Carnegie would be rendering a good service in putting a new building in Snohomish and that he would never have cause to regret it. It is one of the nicest little towns in the West, and its citizenship is composed

PUBLISHING MARKS ON THE CARNEGIE'S FRONT FACADE REPRESENT:
ST. ALBANS PRESS, GERARD LEEU, DENYS JANOT, & WILLIAM CAXTON.

of well-educated, intelligent people." Finally, on March 13, 1909, a letter arrived for Ferguson, offering a $10,000 grant if the city would agree to double their funding of library services to $1,000 a year, as well as provide the site for a new library. The City Council held an emergency meeting on March 19 to affirm the offer and terms of Carnegie's gift.

Construction began within the year. Two young architects, both recent graduates from the University of Pennsylvania, secured the commission for the building. Frederick Thomas Bigger and James Smyth Warner began their careers in Seattle in 1908. Their first project was a residential home in Madison Park.* By 1910, upon completing the Snohomish Carnegie, they had returned to Philadelphia.

The firm of Layton & Meismer was contracted as the builder, overseen by foreman Peddiplace. Work commenced in August 1909, though it paused briefly in September when rumors of shoddy workmanship reached the Library Association. Supposedly,

---

* Bigger became a well-known city planner, serving on the National Capital Planning Commission from 1948 to 1954. He passed away in 1963. Sadly, Warner died just four years after completing the Carnegie, at age 32. He suffered from fatal complications following surgery to remove his appendix. The home in Madison Park is located at 3620 East Prospect Street, Seattle.

the ratio of cement to gravel in the concrete being used was only 6:1, rather than the 12:1 ratio the building's plans designated. Despite this setback, construction concluded by November 1909.

The design followed a prototype typical of Carnegie libraries and civic structures. While Carnegie did not dictate floor plans, he did require certain features like an accessible central stair, high ceilings, and oversized windows to maximize natural light. The simple rectangular form and symmetry reinforced the democratic aspirations of early public libraries and the concept of spiritual elevation through education.[*]

On a quiet day in late January 1910, librarian Mary Mitchell welcomed the public into the new library space. Residents were awed by the lofty and light-filled reading room, with 17-foot ceilings and fir floors. The interior offered 2,160 square feet across its main floor, basement, and small loft. It came equipped with a help desk, a children's corner, and a wide selection of reference books, maps, and archival documents.[**] Magazine racks and community bulletin boards sat beside a cloak room, lavatory, and public telephone. Down below was a spacious meeting room and offices, while above the front entrance, on a balcony, sat a small work desk for restoring damaged books and periodicals. Beside it sat the oldest books, still bearing their original "ATHENEUM" stamps.

The exterior was a stucco concrete painted in creamy white and embellished with blue and terracotta-colored press marks from prestigious publishing houses. This decorative motif, once

---

[*] Carnegie's favorite motto, "Let there be light," was often painted in Carnegie libraries.

[**] The Snohomish High School's advanced manual training class generously donated eight hand-built oak study tables for use in the reading room.

popular in architectural and textile design, gave the building a sense of well-cultivated literacy.

The formal dedication ceremony for the Snohomish Carnegie happened in April 1910. As the new library could only accommodate 25 seated guests, attendees gathered at the Alcazar Theatre down the street. Funds raised at the event helped pay for additional wiring and electric fixtures for the library. Governor Marion Hay and other political leaders praised Snohomish's community activism and progressive ideals.

* * *

Growth & Resilience

In its first decade, the library flourished, growing its collection to over 4,000 books and averaging a monthly circulation of nearly 1,600 books. A children's story hour was introduced, running every Saturday from 11 a.m. to noon, as well as a summer reading club, wherein kids earned a certificate if 12 books were successfully completed. The basement meeting room brought steady rental income and was used frequently by community groups, including the local Grand Army of the Republic, the Snohomish Camera Club, and the Camp Fire Girls. Soon, the head librarian was able to employ an assistant librarian and a custodian.[*]

In 1912, the Cosmopolitan Club officially stepped down from supporting the library to focus on other public benefits. By that time, the library was being sustained by taxes, book fines, rental fees, as well as fees paid by patrons living outside city limits. The library also continued to receive generous donations. In 1926, it received a substantial endowment of $3,500 from the estate of John Watterson Miller, the former postmaster, city attorney,

---

[*] The custodian during the 1920s, Levi Whitbeck, made a salary of $35 per month. The identities of Carnegie custodians are hard to find, though 1968 records note great work done by Mr. & Mrs. Lester Troupe.

and proud supporter of the library cause. He had lived with the Patric family in a home across the street and had witnessed the insitution's evolution. The Library Association installed a bronze plaque in his honor.

Other gifts of money and materials came from Eva Comegys, Dr. Harvey Eldridge, E.W. Klein, Margaret McCready, and other Snohomish citizens. Local groups held book drives to raise money for the purchase of new publications specific to their interests. In 1937, the Snohomish Garden Club installed shrubs on the front lawn and added a few books on flowers and plants to the book collection. This was the start of a decades-long partnership, with their donations of plants and bulbs "adding a great deal in the way of beautification."

The Great Depression hit the library hard. It proved to be a cornerstone for the community and served its residents through some of the darkest days Snohomish had yet experienced. The city's annual budget shrunk year over year and by 1935 the Library Association had to make the tough decision to close completely for a few months. Still, the library managed to fund various upgrades during the decade, including replacing the coal furnace with oil heating, adding electrical outlets and an electrical clock, upgrading to a power lawn mower, and installing new cabinets and bookshelves.

The summer of 1940 brought an intriguing new installation to the Carnegie grounds. The Lervick Logging Company was working a homestead near Lake Roesiger, clearing the land of its old growth trees. These ancient specimens provided the highest quality and most profitable lumber products. After a century of intensive logging, the loggers knew that they were amongst some of the last great forest giants. They selected a 12-foot wide, 275-foot tall Douglas Fir tree to be honored and

LOG TRUCKS ON FIRST STREET, BESIDE THE EAGLES BUILDING.
THE LOG IN FRONT WAS INSTALLED AT THE CARNEGIE.

partially spared. Felled by hand, it was divided and loaded onto the trailers of 12 heavy-duty trucks.

During the annual Kla Ha Ya Days parade, the trucks rumbled through town with their massive log sections. They parked along First Street, allowing residents and photographers to enjoy a sight never to be seen again. Then, at 5 p.m., all but one of the logs were driven to the river's edge, tipped into the water, and floated to the mill. The remaining slice was installed on a concrete base at the corner of the library grounds. It remained as a memento of Snohomish's logging heritage, mesmerizing tourists and children with its imposing size and rings dating back over 620 years.

The Carnegie building commemorated its 40th anniversary in March 1950. The Library Board of Trustees hosted an open house, attended by over 125 guests. There was live music from local high school students, fresh floral arrangements from the Averill family greenhouse, and tea service atop a lace-covered library table. The library received many impressive gifts: Sylvia Lenfest, Emory Ferguson's daughter, donated a copy of Snohomish's first newspaper and scrapbooks made by her father; the First National Bank presented an oversized framed image of oxen on a skid road by local photographer Gilbert Horton; and the Crown Portrait Studio gave 100 prints capturing the library's renowned cherry tree. Former librarian Mrs. Patric attended, assisting with refreshments and managing the guestbook. Also present was Charles Bakeman, a pioneer furniture maker whose sister, Mrs. Jackson, donated the original property.

The first half of the twentieth century saw Snohomish touched by the tumult of two world wars, which though fought in distant lands deeply affected residents at home. In 1955, the Fraternal Order of the Eagles, Lodge No.195 generously gifted an American flag and flagpole. Six years later, on Memorial Day, a new monument for the library was unveiled. After discovering they lacked documentation on Snohomish veterans, the local American Legion launched a campaign to do something. Once again, a group of women stepped forward to help, led by Mrs. Joyce Zalewski, wife of the GAR Cemetery caretaker. The group posted notices in newspapers and store windows to compile a comprehensive list of local veterans. Their efforts culminated in the installation of an etched stone monolith, funded through contributions from residents, businesses, and various clubs, including the Garden Club and Snohomish High School student body. Librarian Geraldine Earls wrote that the tribute "added a touch of solemn dignity and pride to our grounds."

* * *

Memorial with names of local veterans from WWI, WWII, and Korea. Bill Reed and Mrs. Charles Burt are placing wreaths at the base of the memorial.

The memorial was removed to the GAR Cemetery in 2012 while the building underwent renovations. On May 29, 2023 it was returned to its home outside the Carnegie Library.

to the people of Snohomish . . .

THIS IS YOUR LIBRARY

1910 to 1966

We have always been proud of our Library, but the community has outgrown it and needs your support in the Bond Election to enlarge its facilities.

ELECTION TUESDAY, NOVEMBER 8th
7:00 A.M. to 8:00 P.M.

FLYER FROM THE 1966 CAMPAIGN FOR A SPECIAL LIBRARY LEVY.

For generations, the Snohomish Carnegie had dutifully served as a library and meeting space for its community. People of all ages were enriched by its diverse collection of books and periodicals. With the dawning of the "Information Age" in the 1960s, the library's role grew yet again to include a catalog of media resources, digital document reproduction, and greater computer access. What once felt like a vast space was now crammed by the robust library programs of the post-war era and an urban population nearing 5,000. Its 10,000-book and 25-person capacity was woefully inadequate.

Under the leadership of Mrs. Neil Tronsrud and L. Emmett Smith, the library's Board of Trustees spearheaded efforts for a larger space. A $150,000 Special Library Bond Levy appeared on the 1966 ballot. Mrs. Earls emphasized in her year-end report: "New borrowers and increasing requests by local school children, college students, and industrial workers make it mandatory that we have more space and additional facilities if we are to provide adequate service for our growing community."

The levy passed, though it appeared again the following year on a special election ballot. Improper ballot wording had nullified the previous results. The public readily voted in favor once again in September 1967. With construction and maintenance costs secured, a grant of $19,782 from the Washington State Library Commission was set aside to help purchase furnishings for the new space.

After exploring several different designs, Everett architect Harry E. Bostesch was commissioned to create a one-story, flat-roofed, steel-framed addition. Constructed to the south of the existing Carnegie, it expanded the library's capacity to 20,000 books and 55 people. The "Annex," as it was called, opened its doors on September 16, 1968. "The people's response to the building has been most gratifying," read the librarian's report.

The new addition bypassed Carnegie's democratic entry stair, now deemed cumbersome, in favor of street-level access. Linking the old with the new was an enclosed corridor, erasing the original entry and decorative front facade. The annex tripled the floor space and featured floor-to-ceiling windows, flooding the area with natural light and outdoing the Carnegie's original windows. Dark gray carpeting covered the fir floors, reflecting a more contemporary aesthetic. The Carnegie reading room became a children's section, while the offices and meeting room remained below. Modern slim-line shelving, desks, and chairs adorned the new annex. An open house and dedication ceremony on April 27, 1969 drew over 200 people, including guest speaker Maryan Reynolds, the State Librarian.

In September 1971, the Snohomish library board made the decision to contract for service with the county system, Sno-Isle Regional Libraries. Discussions around merging with Sno-Isle had surfaced as early as 1947, when library expenses began to outpace city tax revenue. Joining with the larger county system promised increased access to a broader range of books, reduced maintenance costs, and the ability to hire more library staff. While some patrons opposed the idea, believing the city library should operate independently and preserve its identity, the allure of growth and cost-saving prevailed.

Shortly after the merger, in 1973, Snohomish celebrated the centennial anniversary of its library services, honoring the Atheneum Society. Library staff created a float for the annual Kla Ha Ya Days parade, organized a book sale on the Carnegie grounds, and hosted tea in the reading room during the annual Tour of Homes. In April 1976, as the nation celebrated its bicentennial, the Snohomish Carnegie was officially designated a historic building, part of the Snohomish Historical Society's efforts to secure a spot on the National Register of Historic Places.

* * *

Constructed at a cost of $50,000, the new annex was finished just as the school year started.

Plans for Scheme G from Boyle Wagoner Architects.

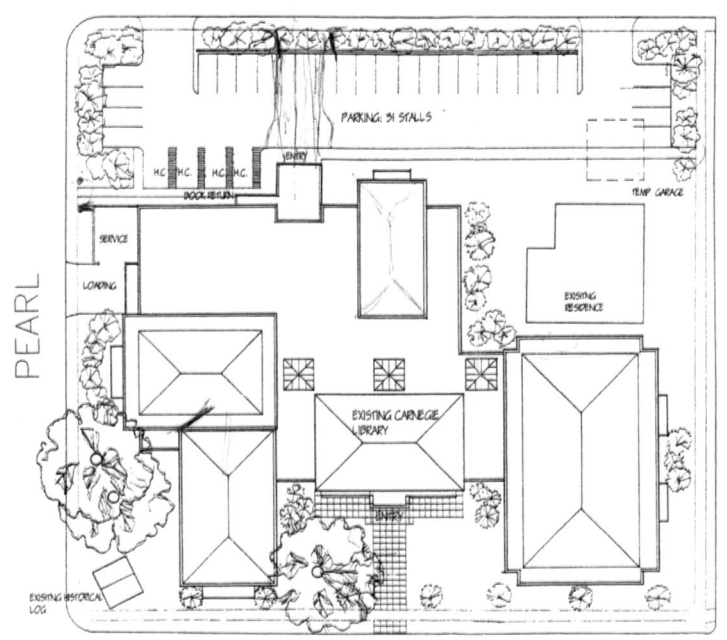

Modern Changes

Water damage, falling ceiling tiles, dirty air vents: this was the state of the Carnegie annex by the early 1990s. Years of heavy use in damp conditions led the midcentury materials to deteriorate, plaguing staff members with moldy air and minor injuries. One Sno-Isle employee experienced a ceiling tile unexpectedly crashing into his head. The issues surfaced while the addition was still new. The City's building manager raised concerns about the lack of slope on the roof and standing water during the winter. The original contractor blamed a lack of supervision. Bostesch, the architect, blamed the contractor.

Meanwhile, the library found itself once again outgrowing its space. The city solicited expansion proposals from architects, with some calling for a demolition of all structures within the Pearl, Maple & Cedar block to make way for a larger library complex. Others looked to undeveloped properties farther afield. In 1998, the City Council approved "Scheme G" from Boyle Wagoner Architects, a dramatic re-engineering of the block. The plan involved removing all the residences along Maple Avenue and replacing with a 21,000 square foot addition. The original Carnegie would be partially preserved at the heart of the new structure, with its front facade restored and the remaining three walls opened into new wings. However, the Design Review Board strongly rejected the proposal, stressing the historic value of properties like the Jackson Row, a set of late 19th-century connected homes built by steamboat scion Daniel Jackson. They urged the city to preserve the small town scale along First Street.

The city resolved to leave the Carnegie building as it was and develop a new library elsewhere. In 2003, Sno-Isle opened a new 23,000 square foot campus north of downtown on the former site of the Northern Pacific railroad depot. The Carnegie sat empty while the city debated its future. With the cost of maintenance

Melody Clemans, Wendy Poishberg, and Mac Bates restore a 1915 chandelier donated by the Everett Carnegie Library.

and repairs escalating, various options were considered. Selling the building to a private developer would bring money in and take the problem off their hands. City Manager Larry Bauman felt such actions were too drastic for "the jewel of Snohomish." Bauman said, "There were those in the community who wanted to tear it down and use the space for parking. I thought that was crazy. This was our town, our library."

Bauman invited the public to present ideas. A small group of residents formed the Carnegie Library Preservation Council. They presented a proposal that restored the exterior and interior back to its original architectural design. The space could then be used as a general-purpose rental facility, with its grounds serving as a park. Other residents championed the idea of a museum, while the school district proposed an alternative high school.

The city endorsed the Preservation Council's proposal. In June 2005 the committee reorganized as the Snohomish Carnegie Foundation, with Melody Clemans at the helm. Over the next two decades, the Foundation's board and volunteers, alongside city staff, invested thousands of hours into advancing the restoration of the building. They pursued numerous grants and fundraising sources in order to amass the more than $3 million needed for the project. An early milestone was a $1 million FEMA grant to fix structural damage the building sustained during the 2001 Nisqually Earthquake. Combined with pre-existing concerns, small cracks and leaks threatened the integrity of the entire complex.

In February 2008, the City Council voted to demolish the annex. Necessary upgrades would have cost upwards of $600,000 and the addition's repair was deemed not worth the expense. The annex found temporary use as a thrift shop and later as the gallery for Arts of Snohomish.

In 2011, BOLA Architecture & Planning, a historic preservation-focused firm, presented a master plan that removed the annex, restored the grounds, and brought the building up to modern ADA standards. The estimated budget had ballooned to $4 million. The following year, seismic retrofitting was completed, including adding a new tile roof, rebuilding the soffits beneath the eaves, and removing the stairs to the former loft workroom.

In 2017, the library was officially shut down by the city and two years later major construction began. ARC Architects led the final designs, which, after demolishing the annex and entry corridor, rebuilt the the front facade and repainted the exterior in a bright shade of "Hubbard Squash." A 7-foot tall crystal chandelier was donated by Purdy & Walters Funeral Home and installed in the former reading room. Made in 1915 of over 1,000 Czechoslovakian crystals, it had originally hung in the Everett Carnegie, but was removed in the 1930s when that library was converted to a mortuary. Now, once again, it was at home in a Carnegie library.

In May 2021, the Snohomish Carnegie reopened its doors to the public, marking a new chapter in its storied history. No longer a library, its revitalization as an event space offered a fresh opportunity for residents to come together. The Carnegie welcomed diverse uses from Holi festivals to drag shows to antique bicycle conventions, reflecting the changing face of the Snohomish community and establishing itself as a venue of continued relevance and vibrancy.

Since its beginning, the Carnegie has been a focal point for gathering and community engagement. With the restoration of the large lawn out front, this tradition has been reignited. The picturesque setting is home to the weekly Snohomish Farmers Market, as well as concerts, holiday festivals, and nonprofit fundraisers. The historic Carnegie grounds offer a hub for the downtown business district of modern Snohomish.

The last century made clear that the significance of the building extends far beyond physical walls. The legacy of the Carnegie endured, not only as a beloved memory bank for generations of patrons, but as a testament to literacy, education, and civic engagement throughout the decades. In honoring history and embracing reuse, the Snohomish Carnegie Library stands as a testament to the forward-thinking vision of its people and city, confirming its heritage and cultural value will be shared with generations to come.

* * *

Members of the Snohomish Carnegie Foundation in 2021, including Mac Bates, Remi Cano, Dan Reynolds, Clara Grager, Melody Clemans, Anne Eason, Terry Lippincott, Renee Deierling, and Candace Jarrett.

Librarian Biographies

Eldridge Morse

Born April 14, 1847, in Wallingford, Connecticut. He arrived in Snohomish on November 1, 1872. Known for his diverse intellectual pursuits, he worked in various professions throughout his life, including law, farming, publishing, politics, and business. He is best known for operating the county's first newspaper, The Northern Star. As one of the founders of the Atheneum, Morse also served as the first official librarian in Snohomish, beginning in 1873. He married his first wife, Martha Turner, in April 1871. Tragically, she became one of the first white women to die in Snohomish, at the young age of 25 from an unknown illness. Morse remarried to Fannie Oliver in 1877. After a divorce, he wed again to Alice Mathews. Morse passed away on January 6, 1914.

Emma Patric

Born May 29, 1877, Emmeline Eleanor Crueger, in Wisconsin. She relocated to the Puget Sound with her parents and nine siblings, where her father found work in mining. Emma attended the University of Washington and her yearbook noted her "especially proficient in German." In June 1901, she married Arthur Patric, a school teacher. Emma was the first recorded librarian for the Women's Book Club, tending to the collection even before the library was formed. She welcomed her first son, John, in May 1902, while living in the apartment attached to the Jackson house library. Daughter Maude arrived in 1904, followed by son Jim in 1906. The family moved across the street to 114 Cedar Street, where they later established a hardware store. Two more children, Dorothy and Bill, completed their family. Emma died in June 1961.

Grace Pineo

Born October 1877, Grace Maude Foster, in Bristol, Maine. In December 1897, she married Louis Pineo and the couple welcomed their son Newell George just four months later. The family lived at 2953 Pine Street, a fitting address given their surname. Louis worked as a brakeman on the railroad. By 1910, Grace and Louis had expanded their family to include four more children. They also relocated to Seattle. The exact dates of her tenure as librarian are unknown, but it is likely to have been no more than a year or two following Emma Patric's resignation.

Mary Mitchell

Born 1872, Mary Lenora Tidball, in Viola, Illinois. She married David Mitchell in June 1895 in Snohomish. He was a millwright who later became chief engineer at the Lowell paper mill. David passed away in April 1904 from tuberculosis, aged 36, leaving Mary to care for their daughter, Doris. Though lacking formal training as a librarian, Mary accepted the job in 1907 and served until 1921. That same year, Mary remarried to George Westgate, a carpenter, and they resided at 6 Union Avenue. She died from kidney failure on April 4, 1944.

Doris Mitchell

Born May 18, 1899, in Lowell, Washington. Doris was eight years old when her mother, Mary, became a librarian in Snohomish. Inspired, she began her career as an assistant librarian in Marshfield, Oregon, then worked as a telephone operator back home in Snohomish. When her mother resigned from her position, Doris seized the opportunity to take over as librarian. Doris served for two years, from October 1921 to September 1923. Receipts show she earned $60 per month, equivalent to about $1,040 today. Doris left the job to attend the University of Washington. After graduating, she worked at the Seattle Public Library for an impressive 42 years. Doris never married or had children and died in June 1978.

Catherine McMurchy

Born August 1870, in Ontario, Canada. She emigrated to Cass County, North Dakota at six years old. The oldest of eight children, Catherine worked as a schoolteacher in the small town of Reed, ND. In 1909, she moved to 429 Cedar Street in Snohomish, along with her parents and sisters. She continued teaching grade school while pursuing library training in Everett. In 1923, Catherine accepted the librarian position in Snohomish. She served 17 years before resigning due to ill health. By 1950, her health had declined further and her sisters helped her relocate to a nursing home in Seattle. She died of a stroke on January 26, 1956 and was laid to rest in Evergreen-Washelli cemetery. Unfortunately, there was no money in her estate for burial expenses, so King County covered the cost of $91. They left no marker on her grave. In 2001, cemetery vice president Paul Elvig learned of her story from Snohomish residents. He donated a black granite stone and Mike Malone, a librarian with Sno-Isle, initiated a fundraiser to pay for the engraving. Thanks to the contributions of library patrons and other donors, Malone collected $360 and was able to finish the marker.

Ethel Cloes

Born 1889, Ethel Louise Selder Keefe, in Minneapolis, Minnesota. She came westward with her parents, who opened the Superior Bakery on First Street, in a building next to the Wilbur Block. On July 24, 1914, Ethel exchanged vows with Harry G. Cloes in a beautiful ceremony in her parent's home at 212 Avenue D. The wedding was "prettily decorated in roses, dahlias, and Shasta daisies." Harry was a former miner turned deputy marshall, often stationed in Cordova, Alaska. The couple had one daughter, Margaret, born in 1921. The family lived at 123 Avenue E. Ethel supplemented her role as a mother with a career as a teacher at the Riverside School. She turned to librarianship in March 1939. In December 1942, she resigned and moved to Beverly Hills, California to live with her daughter. She died in 1955.

Marie Sweet

Born November 13, 1879, Frances Marie Sweet, in London, England. After a brief stint working in a library in Herne Bay, England, she ventured to British Columbia in her twenties to pursue nursing. Later in her career, she became the superintendent at Aldercrest Sanitarium in Snohomish, making significantly more money than the average woman of her era. This allowed her to buy a house at 412 Glen Street. After 23 years with Aldercrest, she applied for the librarian job on a whim, hoping "to spend more time at home." Her term began in November 1942. During her tenure, she introduced an after-hours book return and installed window shades to comply with "dimout" regulations enforced during World War II. In February 1946, Marie was suddenly struck by chest pains. She was rushed to the Snohomish General Hospital and spent three weeks under medical care. She died of a blood clot in her heart on March 23, 1946.

Mildred Dean

Born August 27, 1884, in Rice Lake, Wisconsin. Her journey as a librarian began around 1905 in her home state, later becoming a children's librarian in Davenport, Iowa. In 1936, Mildred moved to Maui, Hawaii where she served as the "playground supervisor" at Mauna'olu Seminary, a boarding school for mixed race girls.

By March of 1946, Mildred had returned to the mainland and accepted the role of librarian at the Snohomish Carnegie. She lived just across the street at 119 Cedar Street, Apartment 3, in the former Adell Thompson home. Newspapers reported that Mildred consistently took her annual vacation each July in Eau Claire, Wisconsin, visiting her family. During this time, the library was closed to the public. In September 1954, she left Snohomish with plans to move to San Jose, California with her sister, Leora. Mildred died of heart disease in a nursing home in Medford, Oregon on July 14, 1963.

Geraldine Earls

Born October 27, 1903, Geraldine Roddy, in Union, Nebraska. In 1936, she moved to Snohomish with her husband, Stuart Earls, and their son Gerald. Stuart, a fellow Nebraskan, found work with the Federal Packing Company in Everett. A serious accident left Geraldine solely responsible for supporting the family. She initially found work at the G.N. Turner Canning Company, then as a teacher for the Snohomish School District's preschool program. She briefly served as a library assistant in Snohomish, then sought a new job at Paine Field, where a library was being set up for WWII airmen and factory workers. She got the job and reported that her daily routine included "attack alert drills, wearing helmets, and donning a gas mask to cross the street to another building." Afterwards, she was appointed to the Snohomish library board and eventually became the librarian when Mildred Dean retired. Geraldine dedicated 16 years to the Snohomish Carnegie, from 1954 to 1971. She died on September 4, 1996.

Lillian Trapp

Born August 31, 1907, Lillian Martha Henning, in Snohomish. She graduated from Snohomish High School in 1926. In 1930, she found employment as a live-in maid for the Ghiglione family in Seattle, owners of A.F. Ghiglione & Sons' pasta factory. One month shy of her due date, Lillian sued August G. Ghiglione, then King County's deputy coroner, claiming he was the father of her unexpected child and should pay child support. Ghiglione denied it. Lillian gave birth to her son Michael George on June 25, 1936.

Lillian married Arthur August Trapp, a logger, on September 3, 1937. They had a son, David, in 1943. In 1945, she became the assistant librarian in charge of the children's section. In February 1971, she was promoted to head librarian. Following her career at the Snohomish Carnegie, Lillian briefly worked as a kindergarten teacher at Zion Lutheran School, where she also established that school's library. She died September 20, 2005 in Lake Stevens.

Evalyn Klein

Born 1920, Evalyn Jane Boggs, in Napa, California. After graduating high school, she moved to San Francisco to pursue her passion for music, particularly the piano. In 1945 she came to Seattle and started working as an administrative assistant in a law firm. In March 1947, Evalyn married Max Klein, a young attorney who had grown up at 124 Avenue D in Snohomish. A few years later, the couple moved to a more spacious Victorian home at 223 Avenue A. The couple had two children, Phil and Gordy. Evalyn stayed active in church and social clubs, including the Snohomish Study Club, Business & Professional Women's Club, and Lady Lions. She was appointed head librarian at the Carnegie in September 1972, serving until her retirement in the 1980s. She died July 3, 2016 in Snohomish.

* * *

Supplementary

These photos and documents are shared courtesy of the University of Washington Libraries, City of Snohomish, Snohomish Tribune, Sno-Isle Regional Library, the Snohomish Historical Society, the Carnegie Corporation, and Candace Jarrett.

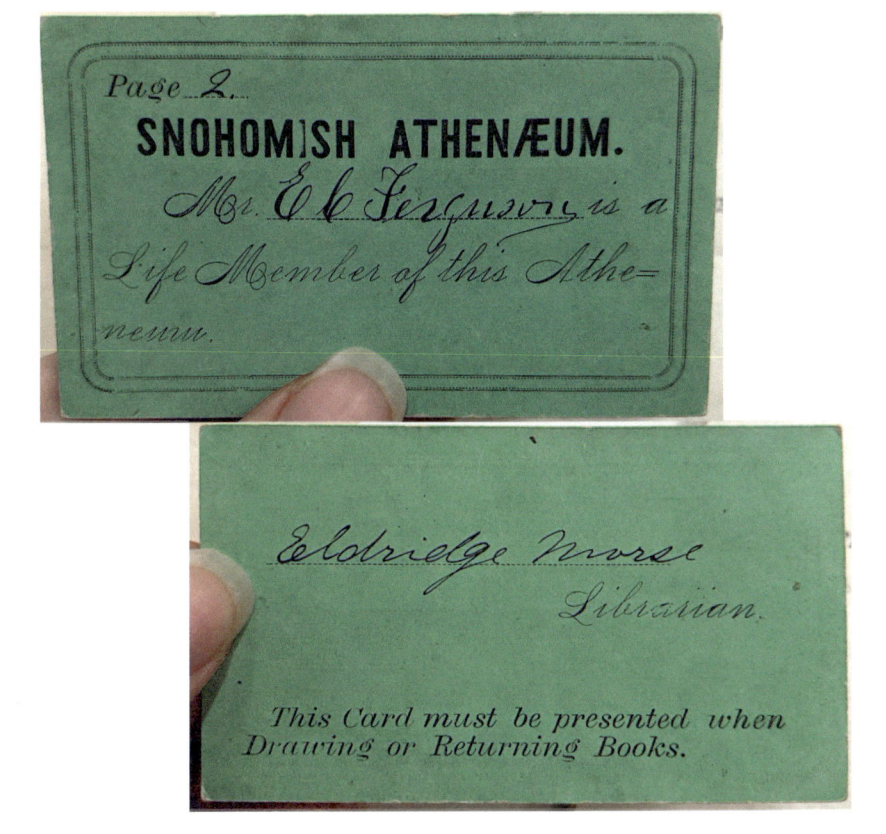

Atheneum membership card, Emory Ferguson.

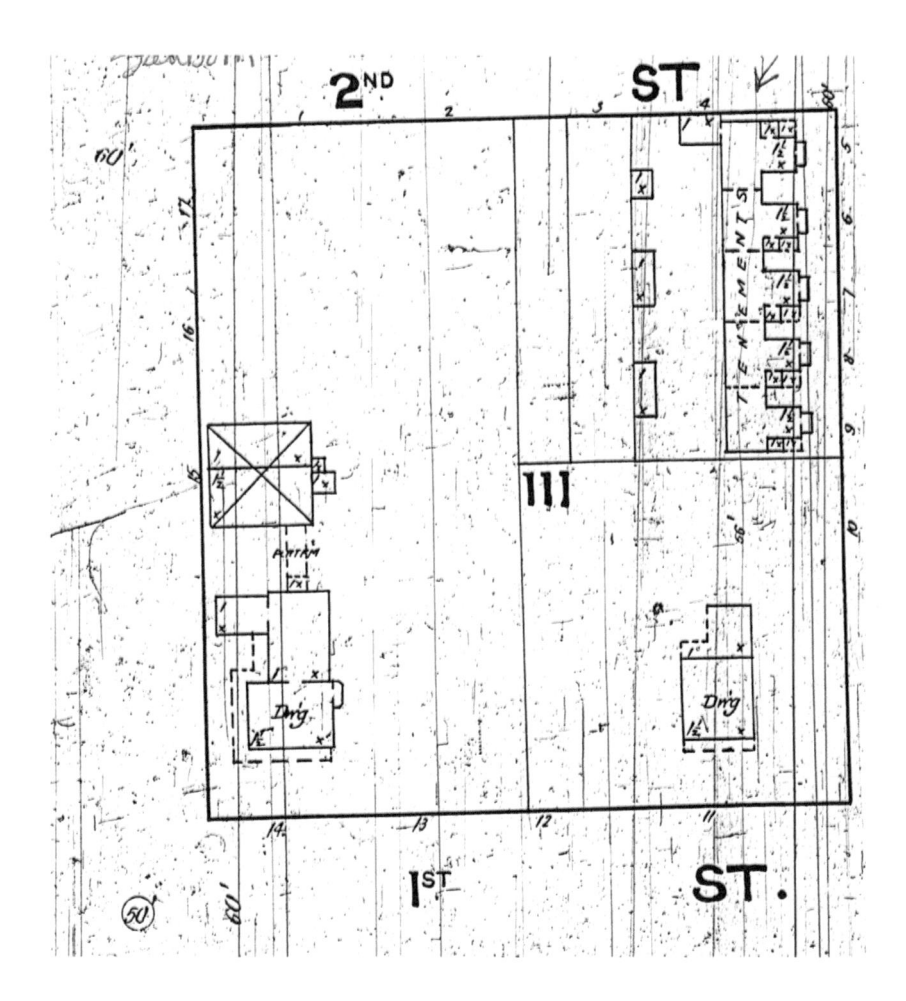

1890 Sanborn insurance map with the Jackson house.
Pearl Street was formerly labeled Second Street.

MONEY-PRODUCERS
Always on Hand and
for Sale by

John E. McManus

EVERETT, WASHINGTON.

232　　　　R. L. POLK & CO'S

SHIP CHANDLERY, Ammunition, Blasting Powder, etc.

SNOHOMISH CIGAR FACTORY, K. & T. PROPRS.

Only Factory in the State that makes a specialty of
HAND-MADE CIGARS.

J

Jackman Henessey, bartender, rms w s Ave C bet 2d and 3d.
Jackson Miss Addie, bds H F Jackson.
Jackson Charles F, Capitalist, res 1st s w cor Maple.
Jackson Frank L, messenger W U Telegraph Co, bds H F Jackson.
Jackson Henry F, Agt P S and A Steamship Co, res cor 1st and Cedar.
Jackson L Medora, clerk county auditor, rms Ave B bet 2d and 3d.
Jackson Wm, messenger Pacific Postal Telegraph Co.
Jacob David J (D J Jacob & Co), res San Francisco, Cal.
Jacob D J & Co, Proprs City of Paris, Hagarty Blk n s 1st.

1893 POLK DIRECTORY SHOWING CHARLES AND
HENRY JACKSON LIVED ACROSS THE STREET.

THE JACKSON LIBRARY-HOUSE, DURING DECONSTRUCTION.
NOTE THE FINISHED CARNEGIE LIBRARY AT FAR RIGHT.

To the Honorable Mayor and City Council:

We, the undersigned citizens of Snohomish convinced that the FreeReading Room is of sufficient service to our town to deserve support, respectfully petition that the sum of fifteen dollars per month from the city treasury be awarded ~~to the Hiyuwawa club to assist them in maintaining it.~~ for its support.

[signatures]

PETITION SIGNED IN SUPPORT OF FUNDING A PUBLIC READING ROOM, SEPTEMBER 1900.

Snohomish, Wash., Oct. 6, 1906.

Mr. Andrew Carnegie,
   New York, N.Y.

Dear Sir:—

On behalf of the people of Snohomish, I again appeal to you for assistance in the erection of a new library building in this city.

In support of our claim as to population I am sending you a signed petition which represents a house to house canvas on the part of the ladies interested in the maintance of our library.

You will note that this petition shows a population of 3396 within our corporate limits, and there were undoubtedly a considerable number who were overlooked.

The city owns one-half block of ground exclusively for library purposes. The building thereon which is used for a library was erected in 1875 and is therefore in very poor condition and must necessarily soon be torn down. We have expended considerable of our income in making repairs until we have reached that point where it seems repairs can no longer be made.

I have the statement of the assistant State Librarian, that no town or city in this state of like population, has done more for library purposes than the City of Snohomish.

We are financially unable to erect a new building and therefore appeal to you for assistance.

Very respectfully,

W. O. Dolsen
Chairman Library Board

LETTER OF THE LIBRARY BOARD'S SECOND APPLICATION TO CARNEGIE, OCTOBER 1906.

SNOHOMISH PUBLIC LIBRARY
Bigger & Warner, Architects, Seattle

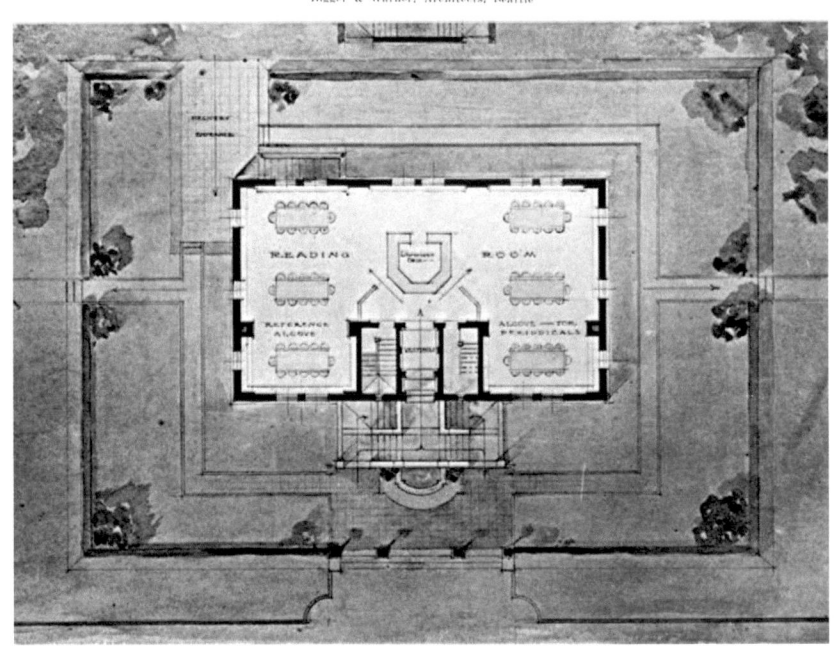

ORIGINAL PLANS FROM BIGGER & WARNER ARCHITECTS.

WOMEN INSTALL REST ROOM

A Rest Room for women at the Library was opened Monday. It was furnished by the ladies of the Snohomish Library Association.

The room is the result of several months discussion and was planned for the use of out-of-town women who are in the city and have no other convenient place to go and for country women who come to Snohomish to shop.

Easy chairs and magazines have been provided and everything has been done to make the hours spent within its atmosphere pleasant.

Several women made special efforts to make the room attractive and comfortable. Mrs. Elizabeth Anderson and Mrs. Ben Barnes contributed the hand worked curtains. The mirror is the gift of Mrs. S. B. Calloway.

JULY 15, 1910, TRIBUNE

LADIES OF LIBRARY START CANVASS FOR MORE BOOKS

Citizens Are Expected to Contribute Liberally

At the meeting of the Library board some time ago the ladies decided to canvass the city for funds to secure the much needed books for the public library, in preference to the giving of entertainments, as has hitherto been done. It was found by experience that the public in general would much rather give the money outright to such a good cause and the many money making schemes were more work than was really necessary.

The ladies have met with much success so far although they are not through yet. The cause is a worthy one and every citizen should encourage the ladies for putting themselves out as they are doing. The library shelves are lacking a great number of books that are necessary for an institution the size of ours and the librarian is the possessor of a long list of helpful books which will be secured as soon as the necessary funds are available.

JANUARY 26, 1912, TRIBUNE

JUST KIDS

Thruout all the days of summer time, and in the evening, too, favorgathering place of Juvenile Snohomish seems to be the library ground. There are no signs, "Keep Off the Grass," or "No Boys Allowed," and young Americans of all ages are free to do there as they please.

Especially is this true on Sunday. In front of the building, or underneath the clumps of trees further away, there will be two or three groups of girls, in their teens, or just out of them, perhaps. There will be popcorn or candy. One of the girls will have a kodak and "shoot" her companions. Then, always near them a few young blades will beg to "get in the picture." Sometimes their request is granted, and the entire crowd sits down again, and one of the boys will go after some more refreshments.

On the side of the library facing First Street there will be a crowd of little girls, doing nothing in particular, but just romping around and chasing each other around Doctor Eldridge's house and back. In a few years they will prefer the front of the grounds to loll upon, but just at present they are contented to play tag by themselves.

Near the fountain and the cherry tree, there will be half a dozen bicycles leaning against the curbs. Some of the owners will be in the cherry tree, picking off the Black Republican cherries that glow in the afternoon sun.

A few paces away—far enough so that the grass is not full of slimy cherry pits—and not too close to the group of misses at the library front, two high school chaps are demonstrating their wrestling ability, with a unaccoutable disregard for clothing that must have cost many weary hours of labor.

Always on the bench that surrounds the tree sit the ones who are most contented. They wish simply to be let alone. On Sunday they are free, and freedom on a lazy summer day means rest. Later on they will take a dip in the Pilchuck,—but not now.

July 9, 1920, Tribune

Memorial on the lawn to honor the passing
of President Warren G. Harding, 1923.

Snohomish, Wash.
April 14- 1923.

W. O. Solsen,
   President of The Library Board,
      Snohomish, Wash.
Dear Sir,
   In case the position of librarian in the Snohomish library should become vacant at any time I hereby make application for that position.
   With regard to my qualifications for the librarianship, - I have studied English and Literature in the University of Minnesota. Later I spent a year in study in the University of Chicago, where I took four quarters of work in English and Literature. This led me to make constant use of the libraries there. Along with my teaching high school English for nearly ten years, the above courses have enabled me to secure a good knowledge of books and reading. I am a graduate of the Washington State College, having received the degree of A. B. from that institution.
   During the current year, in the Everett Public Library I completed the course required there in library training, under Miss Mabel Ashley, the city librarian. I refer you to Miss Ashley for any information you may desire concerning me and my work.
   Should a vacancy in the library occur I shall hope that my application may be favorably received by you and the other members of the Board.
         Very truly yours,
            Catharine McMurchy.
429- Cedar St.

Snohomish, Wash.

August 27, 1921

Snohomish Public Library Board
Mr. W. Q. Dolson, President.

    I wish to make application for the position of librarian of the Snohomish Public Library. I have had ten months experience in Library work under a trained Librarian and can furnish recommendations if desired.

Respectfully submitted,

Doris Mitchell

---

412 - Glen St.
Snohomish, Washington
or
Aldercrest Sanatorium
Snohomish, Washington

October 31st. 1942

Members of the Library Board
  Snohomish Public Library
    Snohomish, Washington.

Gentlemen:
    Hearing there is to be a vacancy at the Snohomish Library, for Librarian, would like to apply for the position.
    I am not a Librarian, but, have had a little experience with books, bookbinding, and repairing. I am sure there is nothing about the work that I could not learn in a short time.
    If my application is considered, I will do my best to co-operate with the Board, and give satisfaction at all times.

Yours very truly

Marie Sweet

APPLICATION LETTERS FROM CATHARINE MCMURCHY, DORIS MITCHELL, AND MARIE SWEET. EXPERIENCE VARIED GREATLY.

```
                              Snohomish, Washington,
                              May 13, 1935


Honorable Chas. G. Bannwarth, Mayor,
City of Snohomish,
Snohomish, Washington.

Dear Sir:

         At a meeting of the Library Board this evening
it was the unanimous decision of the Board that the Library
be closed from June First to September First 1935.

         It is with regret that the Board made the decis-
ion, but due to lack of funds nothing else could be done.

                         Sincerely yours,

                         Secretary Snohomish Library
                         Board.
```

LETTER FROM LIBRARY BOARD TO MAYOR, 1935.

AT TABLE, THE GUEST OF HONOR FOR THE 40TH ANNIVERSARY, EMMA PATRIC. ON THE WALL, A FRAMED PRINT FROM THE FIRST NATIONAL BANK.

SNOHOMISH PUBLIC LIBRARY

SNOHOMISH, WASHINGTON

LIBRARY REPORT 1949

TO THE MEMBERS OF THE SNOHOMISH CITY COUNCIL

The Snohomish Public Library completed its fortieth year of service to the community December 31, 1949. How well it has repaid the taxpayers can not be estimated in dollars nor in figures. Statistics, giving the number of borrowers, the books circulated, reference questions answered and the amount of money spent, show the activities, but can not tell just what the individual borrower gained from the books or from the service given to him. Nor can a report show the goodwill and advertisement it may have brought to your city.

The library was open 290 six-hour days. 15,313 books and 248 magazines were loaned, a total circulation of 15,561.

2,114 borrowers' cards are in force.

52 rural families paid the $1.00 a year fee for the privilege of borrowing books.

```
Route 1    18 families
Route 2     8
Route 3    16
Route 4     6
```
2 families Woodinville route #1, Everett route 2 - 1 and 1 from Monroe.

BOOK STOCK

```
January 1, 1949    -    6,217 volumes
    added by gift           266
    added by purchase       241
    withdrawn                         171
```

Number of volumes at end of year   6,553

Many pamphlets of worth are added yearly. This covers Government and State publications, commercial reports, etc.

The library subscibes for 11 magazines and received 21 gift subscriptions, mostly from Government departments, churches and commercial firms.

Early in the year the Junior Chamber of Commerce sponsored a book drive. The response was generous and very satisfactory. Few books of fiction were given but excellent books in the field of music, art, literature, history and practical science. Books we could not have afforded to purchase.

Through the Interlibrary Loan System all the resources of public and university libraries in the Northwest are made available to borrowers for the nominal fee of postage on the books received. In 1949 Snohomish patrons were loaned 209 books. Their requests covered subjects ranging from architectural plans for a small church to raising chinchillas for profit.

Mildred Dean
Librarian

REPORT FOR JANUARY 1950

Circulation 1,989, eleven under the two thousand mark.

Registration
New borrowers   23 adults
                    8 children
Reregistered   8 adults
                    3 children
Total   42

Borrowers card must be reissued at the end of three years, all inactive cards are withdrawn.

There were three new rural families and one reregistered
Fees $ 4.00
Fines   14.21

18 Interlibrary loan books were received.

REPORT TO CITY COUNCIL, 1949.

```
1952
    The use of the newly decorated
    Auditorium, brought in $162.00
                                        meetings
    Cosmopolitan Club                       4
    Business and Professional
        Woman's Club                        1

    Sportman's Association                 11
    Washington Truckers' Assoc              7
    Canners Union No 780                   13
    Pensioners Union                        4
    Mrs. Forbes Dancing Class              14
    Aldercrest Water Assoc                  1   an annual
    A personal Party (Shower)               1      mtg
    Election   Sno. Co. Credit Assn.        2
                                         1/59
```

1952

Year's circulation of books and magazines

19,630   a gain of   1,275 over 1951

a good increase considering the
number of televisions in the homes –

there has been a decrease in the
junior circulation

REPORTS OF LIBRARY USAGE IN 1952.

OPPOSITE: A LIST OF AVAILABLE MAGAZINES.

64

Current Events and Politics

Current Biography
Look
Newsweek
Saturday Evening Post
U. S. News and World Report

Children and Young People

American Girl
Boy's Life
Highlights for Children
Seventeen
Wee Wisdom

Libraries and Books

A.L.A. Bulletin
Book List
Wilson Library Bulletin

Scientific and Technical

Boeing Magazine
Fortune
Popular Photography
Popular Mechanics
Popular Science
Profitable Hobbies
Flying
Rocks and Minerals
Science Digest
Science News Letter

General

Coronet
Holiday
National Geographic
New Yorker
Parent's Magazine
Today's Health
Your Life
National Education Ass'n
Senior Scholastic
Readers' Digest
America
Arizona Highways
School Arts
Cocker Spaniel Visitor

Homemaking

Better Homes & Garden
Consumer Reports
Good Housekeeping
House Beautiful
Ladies Home Journal
McCall's
Sunset

Outdoor Life

American Rifleman
Nature
Outdoor Life
Sports Afield
Sports Illustrated
World Tennis

Industrial Arts and Educational Vocations

Cross Talk

Literary and Religious

Atlantic Monthly
Columbia (Catholic)
Current Biography
Harper's Magazine
Saturday Review of Literature
National Jewish Monthly
This Day (Lutheran)
Together (Methodist)
Rosicrusian
Theology

Daily Newspapers

Everett Daily Herald) By Subs-
Seattle Times   ) cription

Christian Science Monitor (Gift)

Weekly Newspapers

Snohomish County Tribune (Gift)
Labor Journal (Gift)

Read to Council 5/4/54

SNOHOMISH PUBLIC LIBRARY
SNOHOMISH, WASHINGTON

To the City Council:

The first four months of 1954 have shown several increases in the service of the library to the community. The use of the Auditorium is growing, with an average of ten meetings a month. Three years ago it was used only for the Story Hour period and the Boys' Stamp Club, and by adults on Election Days. The latest organization to hold regular monthly meetings is the Morton's Woman Relief Corps. We are glad to welcome them.

New plumbing in the basement has added to the conveniences; we now can brag of "hot and cold running water" - in the kitchen and in the toilet rooms.

Over 2000 borrowers' cards are in active use. Newcomers to Snohomish are among the most regular borrowers. 91 adults and 43 juniors have been added. 15 Rural families registered. A fee of $1.00 a year per family is asked for out of town borrowers.

6,387 books and magazines were loaned. Summer Reading Clubs are being planned. Mrs. Freal will help with the plans and contact the parents, through the schools.

Friends of the library, and especially the members of the Lady Lions have added many books and magazines for which we are indeed grateful. 68 books were added for circulation, and 45 to the reference section. Mrs. Guy Hubbard gave the Ninth Edition of the Encyclopedia Brittanica, and Mrs. Gordon Bennet 20 vols of Outline of Knowledge. Soon the American Flag will fly daily from the splendid flag staff that the F.O.E. have raised. (By Miss Dean)

REPORT TO CITY COUNCIL, 1954.

INTERIOR VIEW FROM THE LOFT, CIRCA 1954.

68

THE ICONIC CHERRY TREE WAS PLANTED IN THE 1860s. THE CITY CONSIDERED REMOVING IT WITH THE JACKSON HOUSE, BUT EMMA PATRIC "FOUGHT TOOTH AND NAIL... WITH A CRY OF SAVE THAT TREE!" THE TREE SUCCUMBED TO ROT IN 1969. SLICES OF ITS TRUNK WERE MADE INTO POLISHED TABLE TOPS BY LOCAL CRAFTSMAN, FRANK GREEN.

STORY HOUR WAS POPULAR AMONGST YOUNG READERS. VIRGINIA DUBUQUE, READS THE BOOK "CAT STORIES," CIRCA 1956.

Sports, Arts & Crafts, Fairy Tales, Pioneer Stories, and Children of Other Lands rounded out the summer 1958 reading list.

'Twas Friday before Christmas
And at First Street and Cedar
Not many were stirring except one first-grade reader.

He re-arranged the books
And the paperbacks, too;
He straightened the chairs like housemovers do.

"This is a very nice place to be; said he;
We're all by ourselves playing lib-r-ary.
You pick out ~~some~~ books and take out the cards
And deal them all out to a friend named Girard...

"He hides them in books or takes them all home
And the staff blames the mistakes on Willard, the gnome.

"They never get mad--they just shrug and plod on;
You'd think it would daunt 'em,
But they say, 'It's the Tontem.'

"Well, here's to the staff of the book-lending place:
You're all special workers who do your jobs well;
May shelf elves and truants no longer here dwell...

And success and joy be yours next year -
I'll see you around 'cause I'll be here."

                                    A faithful borrower

SAMPLES OF "FAN ART" THE LIBRARY RECEIVED.

Snohomish Public Library

May 13, 1958

Mrs. Nick Angeloff, President
Snohomish Garden Club
Snohomish, Wash.

Dear Mrs. Angeloff,

    It is my pleasure to thank you and members of the Snohomish Garden Club for your wonderfully generous gift of landscaping our Public Library grounds.

    It is a gift which will be enjoyed by so many townspeople as well as travelers passing by.

    While it shows civic pride, it also proves that interested citizens are striving always to improve our community.

    Sincerely,

    (Mrs. H.E,) McCloud, Secretary
    Snohomish Library Board

LETTER FROM LIBRARY BOARD TO THE GARDEN CLUB, 1958.

Art sale in the parking lot, 1970s.

MILITARY GATHERING ON THE CARNEGIE'S FRONT STEPS, CIRCA 1912.

OPPOSITE: THE PROGRAM FOR THE VETERAN'S MEMORIAL DEDICATION, 1961.

SNOHOMISH COMMUNITY MEMORIAL

DEDICATION

MAY 30, 1961 — 11:00 A.M.

"in memory

of those who

gave their lives

that we might live"

THE SNOHOMISH COMMUNITY MEMORIAL

It has been said that God works in minority groups. The establishment of a permanent Memorial to the men of Snohomish who gave their lives in W.W. I, W.W. II and Korea, that we might live, is a clear example of this statement.

The project was started by a handful of people. In the spring of 1960 the members of The American Legion Auxiliary, Earl Winehart Unit No. 96, planned to honor the heroes from Snohomish in a window display, using crosses bearing the names of Snohomish war dead. It was at this time that it became evident that the lists were not in existence. In such a short period of time the names were being lost and forgotten and there was no complete historical record any place in the town. Mrs. Dee Barnhart was appointed to act as General Chairman of a Memorials Committee, by the President of the American Legion Auxiliary, Mrs. Val Zalewski. She was directed to try to establish a permanent Memorial honoring our local heroes. Realizing that such a project would need strength to succeed, other women from other patriotic service organizations were contacted and in the summer of 1960 a small group of women representing their respective Auxiliaries met and formed the original Committee. From this early beginning and with the full backing of the men of the Posts behind the Auxiliary, these people banded together and formed the Snohomish Community Memorial Committee. They were rewarded with the strength that was shown when the people of the community became the underwriters of this project.

SNOHOMISH PUBLIC LIBRARY

SNOHOMISH, WASHINGTON 98290

1966 REPORT

The following sixty-third Annual Library Report is respectfully submitted to Mayor O.J. Wirsching and Members of the City Council.

The library was open to the public 294 days. From 2-8 P.M. Mondays thru Fridays - 10 A.M. - 4 P.M. on Saturdays with the exception of Saturday hours Of 9 A.M. - 1 P.M. during July and August.

New and gift additions to the book stock were as follows:

	PURCHASED Fiction	Non-fiction	Reference	GIFTS Fiction	Non-fic.	Total
Adult	105	179	18	94	103	499
Juvenile	153	47		8	7	215
Total	258	226	18	102	110	714

The cost of the 502 books purchased was $1,578.49, an average of $3.14 per copy. This was an increase of 63¢ per copy over last year. Rebinding expenditures for the year were $124.61, this included the binding of three years of National Geographic issues into six hard back volumes for permanent reference books.
183 books were withdrawn from circulation - these were lost books and those damaged or worn beyond repair.

PRESENT BOOK STOCK IS AS FOLLOWS:

	Fiction	Non-fiction	Reference	Total
Adult	3,771	4,352	987	9,110
Juvenile	2,215	1,068		3,283
Total	5,986	5,420	987	12,393

NEWSPAPERS AND MAGAZINES

We subscribe to three newspapers - The Seattle Times, The Everett Herald and The Sunday Edition of The New York Times.
We receive gift subscriptions to The Snohomish County Tribune, The Christian Science Monitor, The Everett Labor Journal and The Northwest Progress.

We subscribe to sixty-one adult and six children's magazines.
We receive sixty-eight magazines as gifts from library patrons, civic organizations, religious, fraternal, business and governmental sources.

CIRCULATION

	Fiction	Non-Fic.	Magazines	Misc. pamphs,maps, etc.	Total
Adult	17,138	7,407	3,338	238	28,121
Juvenile	11,518	2,688	365		14,571
Total	28,656	10,095	3,703	238	42,692

Our patrons also borrowed 104 books, 13 pamphlets and 1 magazine through our Interlibrary Loan Service Contract with The Bibliographic Center of The University of Washington Library.

BORROWERS:

	ADULT City	ADULT Rural	JUVENILE City	JUVENILE Rural	TOTAL
Registered -(New)	214	134	104	10	462
Re-registered	289	138	26	37	490
Total	503	272	130	47	952
Active '64 - '66	1677	524	482	80	2763

Two hundred- two rural residents paid the annual $2.00 fee for library cards.

1966 will become a commemorative date in Snohomish Public Library history. Due to the combined efforts of The Library Board of Trustees, our Mayor, and City Council Members a $150,000 4-mill bond levy was presented for approval on the Nov. 4, election ballot for the purpose of acquiring funds to remodel the present library building and to add additional new space.

New borrowers and increasing requests by local school children, college students and industrial workers make it mandatory that we have more space and additional facilities if we are to provide adequate service for our growing community.

It is gratifing to know that the local tax payers approved this special bond levy.

In addition to our city officials and library trustees special credit and thanks for the passage of this measure are due to Mr. Bill Bates of The Snohomish County Tribune and Mr. Ned Carrick of The Everett Herald for the effective publicity they gave this project and also to Mr. Hal Moe, Supt. of Snohomish schools for his endorsement and support.

We are grateful to The Friends of The Snohomish Public Library Organization for assisting with the payment of printed campaign material. Our thanks also to The Boy Scouts, The Sno-Gals and many other civic minded individuals who took part in bringing the need of a better library to the attention of the voters.

Mr. Robert C. Jastad, local pharmacist, The Junior Study Club and an anonymous donor have made cash contributions for improved library facilities.

I trust that your 1967 report will be able to announce that the new facilities are or will soon be available to library patrons.

Geraldine L. Earle
Librarian

REPORT TO CITY COUNCIL, 1966.

"A"

NEW (TOTAL)	NEW & OLD
NEW BUILDING AREA — 7000#	ADDITION 4500# 4500#
	EXIST'G 1ST FLR. 2160#
DISADVANTAGES —	EXIST'G BSMT. 2160#
1.) PUBLIC OPPOSITION	8820
2.) TEMPORARY QUARTERS DURING CONSTRUCTION	AREA USED UP IN STAIRWAYS. — 978
3.) NO RENTAL SPACE	7842#
	DISADVANTAGES —
	1.) TWO LEVELS FOR LIBRARIAN TO TAKE CARE OF.
	2.) CIRCULATION OF LIBRARIAN NOT AS EFFICIENT AS POSSIBLE.
	3.) DUMBWAITER REQUIRED FOR CHANGE OF LEVELS
ADVANTAGES.	4.) REPLACEMENT OF EXISTING HEATING SYSTEM.
1.) MAINTANCE.	5.) MAINTANCE.
2.) ARCHITECTURAL CONTINUITY	6.) CONSTRUCTION CONDITIONS OF NEW MEETING OLD
3.) BETTER SITE UTILIZATION	7.)
4.) BETTER PLAN UTILIZATION	

SNOHOMISH PUBLIC LIBRARY
4-16-67

Notes from the Library Board on building pros and cons, 1967.

Opposite, above: a campaign flyer to support the library levy.
Below: architectural plans for the annex.

A Public Library Snohomish Can be Proud Of!

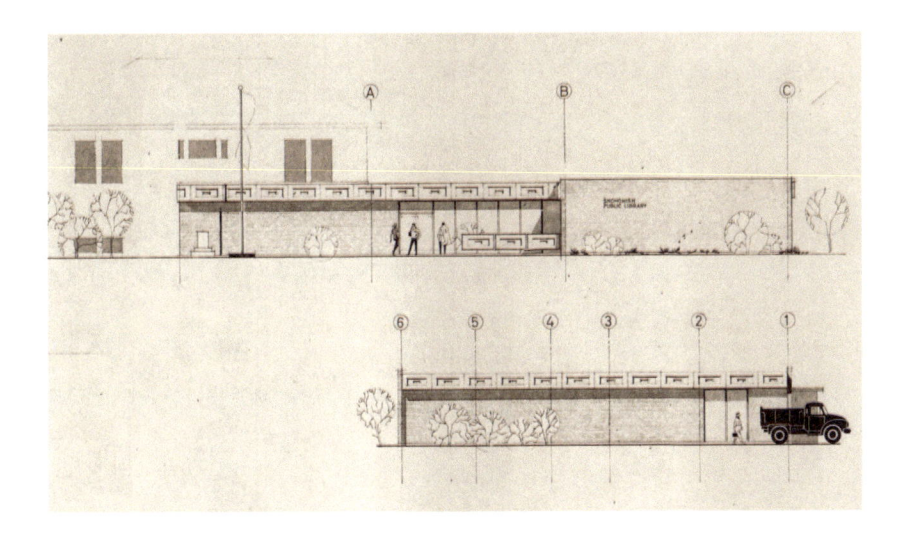

LIBRARY PRESENTATION: Harry Botesch, right, architect, presents library to Mayor Payson Peterson. The mayor accepted the handsome facility on behalf of the people and, in turn, turned it over to the people.
—(Tribune Photo)

GUEST SPEAKER at Sunday's library dedication was State Librarian Maryan Reynolds. She congratulated Snohomish and its library board for taking its responsibilities seriously and outlined the future challenges of the "information explosion."

GERALDINE EARLS WITH NEW SIGNAGE FOR THE ANNEX ADDITION.

OPPOSITE: NEWS COVERAGE OF THE ANNEX DEDICATION, 1968.

DETAIL FROM A THANK YOU CARD FOR CAMPAIGN SUPPORTERS, 1968.

OPPOSITE, ABOVE: THE LIBRARY'S NEW COPY MACHINE.
BELOW: MODERN BOOK AND MAGAZINE SHELVING.

COPY CAT: Joanne Seipp, Snohomish High School student and a part-time librarian, demonstrates the new copy machine installed in the new Snohomish Library. It will copy documents, letters, pages from books, newspapers and other reproducible material. All it takes to operate it is a dime, according to Librarian Geraldine Earls.

Library parade entry for Kla Ha Ya Days, 1969.

MEETING OF THE LIBRARY BOARD IN THE NEW ANNEX, 1970S.

SNO-ISLE REGIONAL LIBRARY
P. O. BOX 157
MARYSVILLE, WASHINGTON
98270

MAE L. SCHOENROCK, LIBRARIAN

November 23, 1971

Ms. Evelyn Lysons, City Clerk
City of Snohomish
Snohomish, Washington 98290

Dear Ms. Lysons:

    Yesterday at our regular meeting, the Regional Library Board signed the contract for library service to the City of Snohomish. A copy for your files is enclosed.

    We are looking forward to working with Snohomish.

                  Sincerely yours,

                    Mae L. Schoenrock
                    Librarian

MLS:dr
Encl.

— Serving Snohomish and Island Counties —

LETTER OF ACCEPTANCE FROM SNO-ISLE REGIONAL LIBRARY, 1971.

OPPOSITE: LIBRARY NEWS COVERAGE FROM 1987.

Your Link to the Past and the Future!

Snohomish library clerk Byron Manering and librarian Becky Buckingham keep busy serving the community at 105 Cedar.

An old resting spot for the young

Five-year-old Lori Fitzthum makes the 620-year-old Douglas Fir in front of the Snohomish Public Library her resting spot as she reads the book, "How Animals Behave." Lori is the daughter of Don and Karen Fitzthum. The landmark tree was felled by the Lervick Logging Company in 1940 in the Lake Roesiger District.

(Les Fetchko photo)

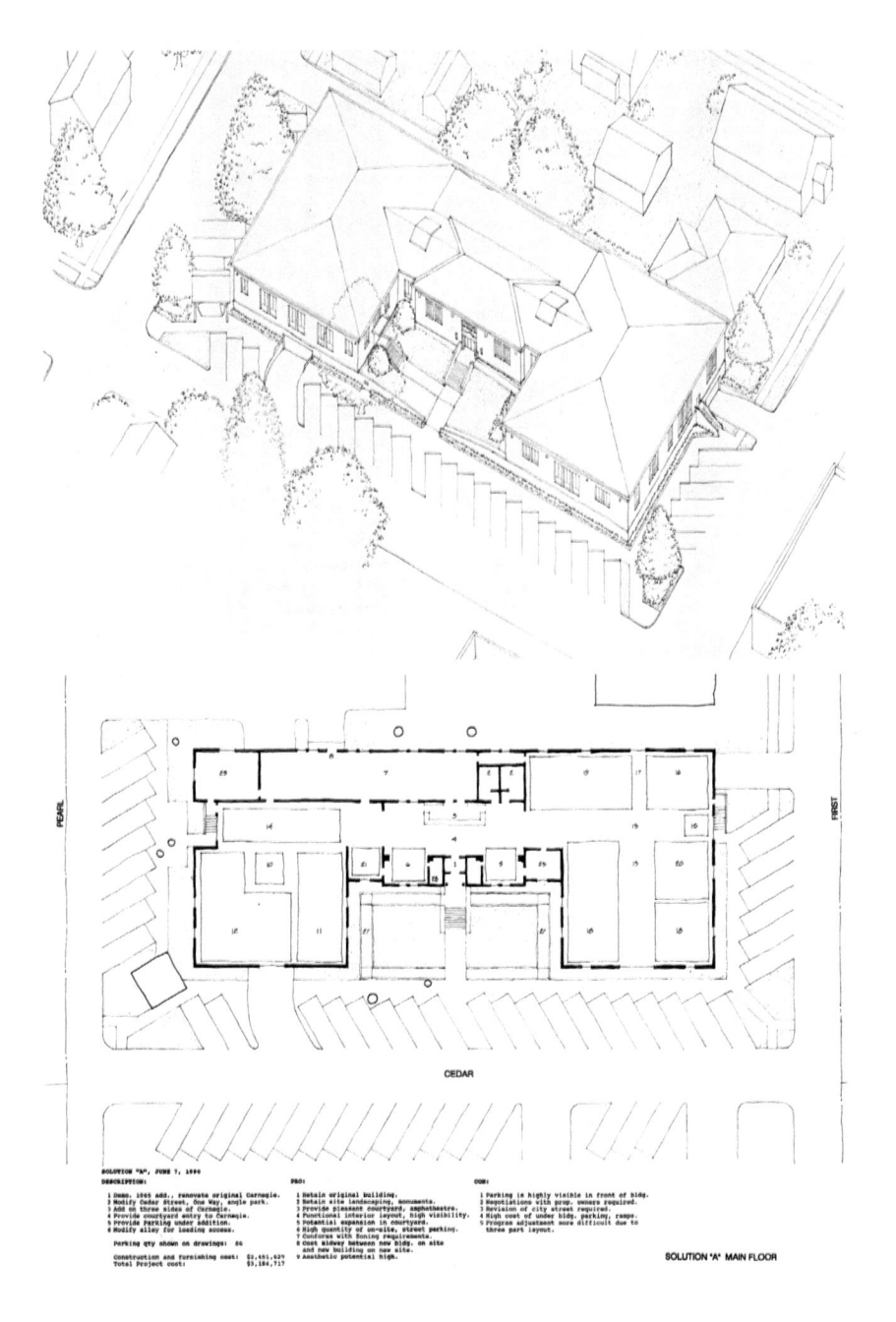

Solution "A" from Johnston Architects, drafted in 1990.

Draft

Memorandum

Date: May 30, 1998
Subject: Library Design
To: City Council
From: Falken Forshaw, Chair
    Design Review Board

Redevelopment of the Carnegie Library site offers a rare opportunity to the City of Snohomish. The Design Review Board urges you to consider fully those historical and neighborhood design issues so critical to the success of this important civic project.

First, some history: The list of officially designated historic structures was not developed as a comprehensive list of contributing structures. The list was prepared to include structures that are representative of the architectural styles present in Snohomish in order to qualify for National Historic District designation. Funds did not exist at the time for a comprehensive study, and one has never been completed. Such a study is critically needed, as this project illustrates.

Design review by the Board is the system currently in place to protect contributing structures, and these are identified on a case by case basis, triggered by development permit application. This occurred for the library at the recommended preliminary stage, with discussions between the architect and the Board, where the contributing nature of three structures in addition to the Carnegie Library was expressed. These structures are the ~~Patrick~~ single family home, the Blackman attached row houses and the brick insurance building.

Second, the Board considers preserving the scale of the existing neighborhood as critical. The bulk of the proposed building, its presence on the street edges, and the layout of over one hundred parking stalls, as well as associated traffic impacts, must acknowledge and reflect existing conditions. Creating drastic changes would destroy those historical and visual values recommended for preservation and protection in the Community Development Plan and which are the purpose of the National Historic District.

The Design Review Board appreciates any opportunity to contribute to this much-needed library, and look forward to continued involvement in the design process. Thank you for your consideration.

CC: Library Board
    Bill McDonald, City Manager

LETTER FROM DESIGN REVIEW BOARD TO CITY COUNCIL, 1998.

Exterior of the Carnegie library, circa 2005.

INTERIOR OF THE ANNEX AS AN ART GALLERY, CIRCA 2005.

Is the Snohomish Library
HAUNTED?

See for yourself with
ghostcam

One afternoon a librarian heard footsteps coming from the third story of the Snohomish Library. Since the third floor was used for storage, making it difficult to walk, the librarian was baffled at what the noise could be. At that moment a woman, wearing a hat and blue dress from the 1920s, appeared and began walking down the stairs. The employee followed the woman as she continued walking into the main section of the library, but then she was nowhere to be found.

Ghost?
You decide.

Now, you can visually and virtually capture the fabled Snohomish Library ghost 24 hours a day using ghostcam at **www.heraldnet.com/ghostcam**. If you happen to catch a glimpse of the ghost, send us the image and we'll post it. You can even win a prize for your ghost hot fling skills.

ghostcam debuts today (Friday the 13th) at 11:00 a.m.

We also want to hear about your personal ghost encounters. If you have a ghost story you'd like to share, post it on **www.heraldnet.com/ghostcam** or send it to The Herald, Ghost Stories, P.O. Box 930, Everett, WA 98206. Visit HeraldNet during the next year to read about the ghostly experiences of others.

www.HeraldNet.com/ghostcam

NORTHWEST TELCO CREDIT UNION
www.nwtelco.com

SNO-ISLE REGIONAL LIBRARY SYSTEM
WWW.SNO-ISLE.ORG

ON HALLOWEEN NIGHT 2000, REPORTERS FROM THE HERALD SPENT THE NIGHT. A "GHOSTCAM" STREAMED LIVE ON THE NEWSPAPER'S WEBSITE.

BEGINNING IN THE '90S, THERE HAD BEEN GHOSTLY SIGHTINGS OF A WOMAN DRESSED IN BLUE, AS WELL AS MYSTERIOUS FOOTSTEPS COMING FROM THE LOFT WORKROOM. ONE REPORT CLAIMED A SPIRIT CAUSED A LOUD BANG, ALERTING TO A FAULTY HEATER IN THE LOFT BEFORE IT CAUSED A FIRE.

FORMER LIBRARIAN CATHARINE MCMURCHY LACKED A GRAVESTONE, WHICH "STATISTICALLY SPEAKING, IS THE SIXTH MOST LIKELY CAUSE OF A HAUNTING," SAID MIKE MALONE, A REFERENCE LIBRARIAN WITH SNO-ISLE.

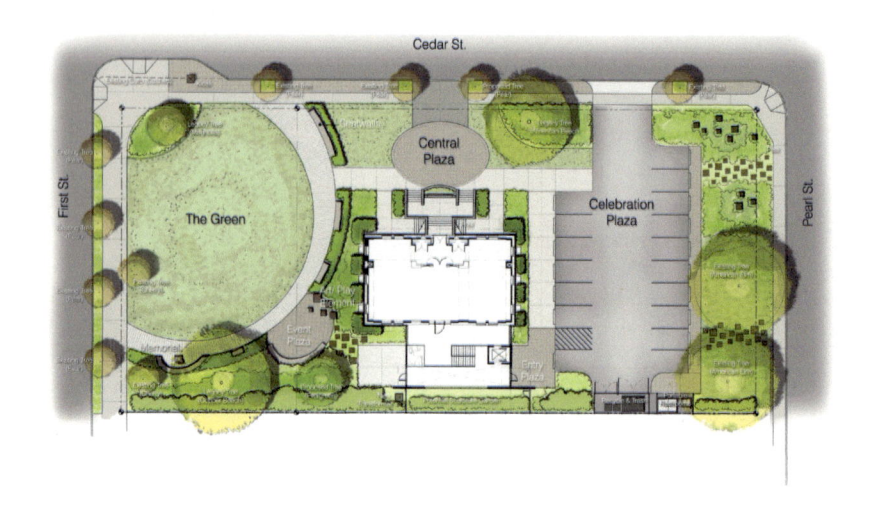

Landscape plan for the new site, 2010.

Opposite: before and after the annex takedown.

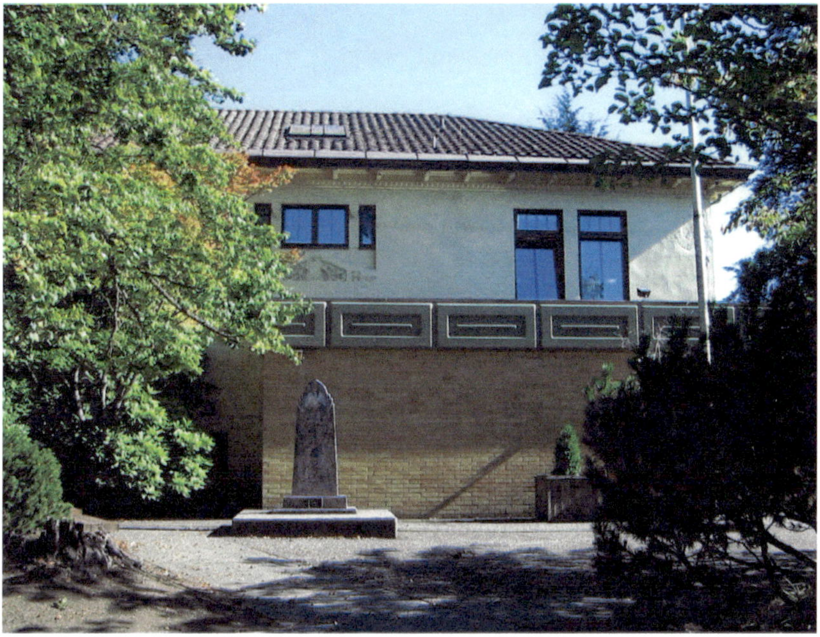

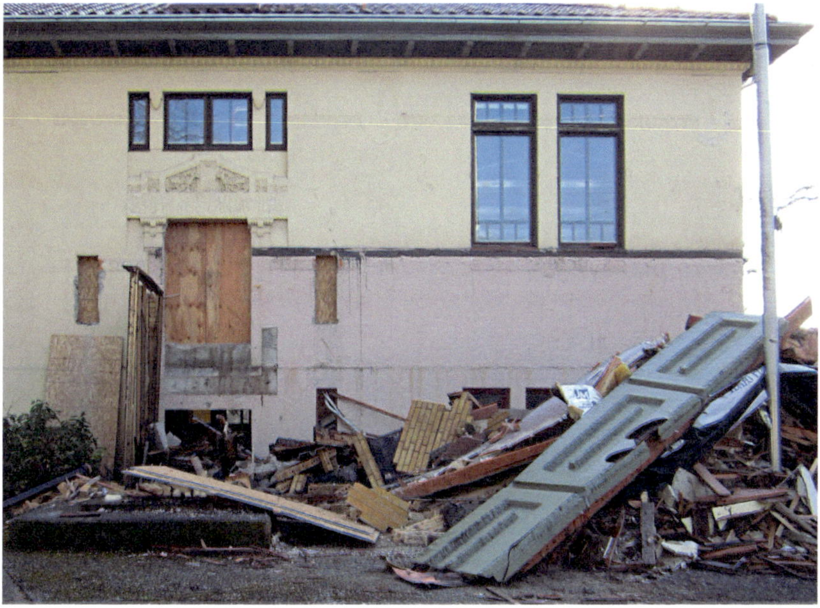

Acknowledgements

Researching and writing this book has been less of a labor and more of a thrill. To document the history of one of Snohomish's most treasured landmarks was an honor.

This would not have been possible without the Snohomish Carnegie Foundation. Their invitation to Trent Deverter and I to produce a documentary film was led by Mac Bates, who saw our passion for creating compelling history and proposed the project to the board. Special thanks to Melody Clemans, Renee Deierling, Candace Jarrett, Terry Lippincott, Dan Reynolds, Cathy Reines, Clara Grager, and Michael Edwards for their unwavering and enthusiastic support. The Foundation's dedication towards the restoration of this local icon has been inspiring.

I am also indebted to historians and writers before me, including Warner Blake and the late (ca. 1939) William Whitfield, whose insights greatly enriched the content of this book.

Gratitude is owed to the Snohomish County Tribune, Everett Daily Herald, Sno-Isle Regional Library, and Snohomish Historical Society for providing access to the archives and information that formed the backbone of this narrative.

Thank you to the City of Snohomish for supporting the renovation process, as well as my research process. Brandi Whitson deserves special mention for the many public records requests she procured for me over the last couple years. (There will be more!) This civic-public-private spirit of collaboration is the reason the renewed Carnegie got a "second act."

Lastly, I am deeply grateful to the volunteers, and Snohomish community at large. Using and loving the Snohomish Carnegie breathes new life into it, ensuring that future generations will continue to benefit from the wisdom of antiquity.

Thank you,

Taylor

Made in the USA
Columbia, SC
14 May 2024